EXPLORER BOOKS

SHARKS

by
Della Rowland

Published by The Trumpet Club
a division of Bantam Doubleday Dell Publishing Group, Inc.
666 Fifth Avenue, New York, New York 10103

ISBN: 0-440-84188-7

Produced by Parachute Press, Inc.
Printed in the United States of America
February 1990

10 9 8 7 6 5 4 3 2 1
CW

For Tony and the Fradkin kids —
Trevor, Hunter, and Alexis

Sincere thanks to the staff
of the Mystic Marinelife Aquarium
for its valuable help.

Chapter One

Strange and Wonderful

What do you picture when you hear the word "shark"? You probably think of the huge, streamlined creature from the movie *Jaws*. Of course some sharks do look like the *Jaws* shark. But many others do not. Sharks come in any number of shapes and sizes. The fact is there are over 350 different kinds of sharks in all.

There is a shark, for example, that has a long, flat nose shaped like a saw. Along the edges of the nose are sharp, sawlike teeth. To catch fish, the *sawshark* slashes at them with its nose.

Another strange shark has a head shaped like the letter T. It is called the *hammerhead shark*. The head is a flat bar about three feet wide, with an eye and nostril at each end!

Still another odd-looking shark has a face covered by a stiff flap that looks like a shovel. A Japanese fisherman was the first to discover this shark. When it caught on his line, the creature looked so frightening that the fisherman named it the *goblin shark!*

Some sharks have strange looks. Others have strange habits. The *nurse shark* curls its side fins down and walks on them like legs. Nurse sharks also pile up on top of each other by the dozens and lie still as if they are sleeping.

The *swell shark* gets its name from the strange way it protects itself. If it is in danger, this shark gulps air or water and swells up. Suddenly becoming twice its normal size, the shark frightens its enemies away.

The smallest shark can be held in a person's hand. The *dwarf shark* is only about six inches long.

The biggest shark grows up to 45 feet. This enormous creature is called the *whale shark.* The mouth of a whale shark is six feet wide and has more than 3,000 teeth. But this shark is a gentle giant. It would even let you hitch a ride on its broad back.

Sharks come in many colors. Some are brown. Some are beautiful silvery blue. Some are spotted. Others are striped. Still others look like checkerboards.

Sea animals called skates and rays may not look like sharks, but they are members of the shark family. These cousins eat the same kinds of food as sharks, have the same kind of teeth, skin, and gills. But many skates and rays have wide, thin bodies shaped like kites. These flat creatures lie on the bottom of the ocean. When food crawls by, they rise up and cover it. Once the crab or lobster has been trapped in this way, the skate or ray can eat it at its leisure.

What Is a Shark?

Even though all members of the shark family don't look alike, they still have much in common. All sharks are fish. All sharks are meat-eaters. They all have a protective skin covering made of sharp toothlike scales. And the skeletons inside their bodies are not made of bone. What kind of unusual creatures are sharks?

Sharks belong to a family of fish called elasmobranchs. Inside this large family, the best known group of sharks is called galeoid. This book describes galeoid sharks most of the time. These are the well known sharks that have long cigar shaped bodies and pointy snouts. They also have a top fin that can be seen cutting through the water. The most famous galeoid may be the *great white shark,* the star of *Jaws.*

Sharks live in waters all over the world. Some swim alone, others travel in groups called schools. Most of them like to swim in water that is fairly warm. And sharks usually live in the open ocean. For example, *mako* and the great white make their homes in deep water far out at sea.

Other sharks live closer to shore, near reefs and rocky areas. Then there are the bottom dwellers, who live on the ocean floor. The *leopard shark* and the nurse shark are both bottom dwellers.

Some sharks are rarely seen because they live in the deepest waters of the ocean. The goblin shark is one of these. Until the Japanese fisherman caught the first, no one knew the species existed.

Just a few years ago, a fishing crew found a new and large deep water shark. It was fourteen feet long and weighed about a ton. Its mouth was huge, so it was named *megamouth*, or big mouth. Scientists discovered that the inside of the shark's mouth was silvery. They believe that the silver mouth glows in the dark. Even in the deep and dark waters where the shark lives, a glowing mouth probably attracts food fish, inviting them to swim inside. The smaller fish would become dinner for the megamouth.

Many sharks move from place to place, or migrate. When the season changes and the weather grows hot, they travel to cooler waters. Some sharks migrate to far places each year, but they always return to the same warm spot to have their babies.

A few sharks have been found in freshwater rivers. This is a mystery to scientists because a shark's body is made to live in the salt water of the oceans. Researchers believe the shark might swim into fresh water to get rid of parasites on its body. These parasites can't live in fresh water.

The *bull shark* is one kind of shark that can swim in fresh water and not be harmed. Years ago, a bull shark swam more than 1,000 miles up the Mississippi River. Today, there are dams along the Mississippi that bull sharks can't get past. But they are still found as far as 100 miles up smaller rivers in Louisiana.

Shark Legends

For many centuries, people around the world have been fascinated by sharks. Over the years they have told amazing stories about these fish. The storytellers believe the tales they tell. But the legends are so old, no one really knows if they are true. Sometimes a shark legend made the creature seem friendly. Other times the shark was the enemy.

In Hawaii, there is a legend about Kama-Hoa-Lii, a god known as the shark king. Kama-Hoa-Lii lived in a cave in the ocean. From there he ruled over the other sharks, protected swimmers, and even guided lost fishing boats home. The king of the sharks was friendly to the island people of Hawaii.

Hawaiians were not the only people who believed sharks protected them. In many countries, children used to be given necklaces made of sharks' teeth to wear at night. The teeth were supposed to protect them from harm and give them good appetites so the children would grow big and strong.

Other people feel they have to protect themselves from sharks. Japanese fishermen wear red cloths around their waists when they dive for shells. The red cloth is supposed to keep sharks away. Pearl divers in Sri Lanka use magic charms to keep sharks from attacking.

In olden times, sailors on whaling ships believed in many shark legends. If a *blue shark* was spotted, they thought it was a sign of death. Sailors who happened to catch a porpoise often nailed the porpoise tail to the side of their ship. Porpoises sometimes kill sharks. The sailors thought the sight of a porpoise tail would keep sharks away from their boat.

Sailors out on the ocean often thought they had spotted a sea monster. In many cases what they saw was probably a school of *basking sharks* swimming near the surface. These giants often travel single file like elephants. The sharks swim with the nose of one shark touching the tail of the one in front. Looking at the sharks from their boat, the sailors could only see fins above the water. To them, the row of fins looked very much like the back of a sea serpent!

Living Fossils

Sharks have been in Earth's oceans for almost 400 million years. The earliest dinosaur only appeared about 200 million years ago. In other words, the shark family is twice as old as the oldest dinosaur. That's why sharks are sometimes called living fossils. Fossils are the remains of a much earlier time.

We know how old these creatures are because scientists have found parts of ancient sharks to study. Shark teeth have been found that are as big as a human hand. Scientists used the teeth to make a model of the jaw of this very old species. When they finished, the scientists found the shark's mouth was large enough to hold a small car! This monster could have swallowed half a dozen people at one time.

Scientists named this ancient shark the *carcharodon megalodon*, which means huge tooth. Scientists believe the great white shark is related to it. Some people who study sharks believe that a few of these giants might still be around. It is possible that huge megalodons may still be living in the deepest parts of the ocean, places where people are not yet able to go.

There are no dinosaurs left today, but there are still many kinds of sharks. One reason sharks have survived is their special shape and design. Every inch of their sleek bodies helps them find food and stay alive.

Chapter Two

A Shark's Body

Maybe you have seen the skeleton of a dinosaur mounted in a museum. You might have seen an ancient bird or fish skeleton, too. Over time, the bones of these animals became hard as rocks. Their skeletons turned to fossils that we can look at today.

But no one has ever found the skeleton of an ancient shark. Why? Because shark skeletons are not made of bone. They are made of cartilage, and cartilage is softer than bone. After an animal dies, cartilage slowly decays and disappears.

Most species of fish have skeletons made of bone. These fish are called bony fish. Sharks are fish, but they are not bony fish. This is one important difference between sharks and other fish.

Cartilage is more flexible than bone. Your ears are made of cartilage. That is why you can bend them. Because its skeleton is made of cartilage, a shark is very flexible. A shark can turn faster and more easily than a bony fish. In fact, a shark can turn completely around in a space that is only as long as its body. To turn, most fish need much more space.

Skin

The skin of a shark is not like that of most fish. Fish are covered with thin, stiff plates called scales. Sharks have scales, but the scales are like tiny teeth. Their skin teeth are even covered with enamel, like the teeth in their mouths. Sharkskin is so rough that years ago people used to dry it and use it as sandpaper.

The skin teeth on a young shark are very small. Eventually the shark outgrows them. Just as baby teeth in children fall out, so do the first teeth on a shark's skin, and bigger ones grow in their places.

Gills

Right behind a shark's head are slits in its skin. These slits are part of the shark's gills. Most fish have only one gill slit on each side of their head. But sharks have five to seven slits.

Like other fish, sharks breathe through their gills. Water enters their bodies through their mouths and goes back out into the ocean through their gills. The gills remove oxygen from

Blue Shark

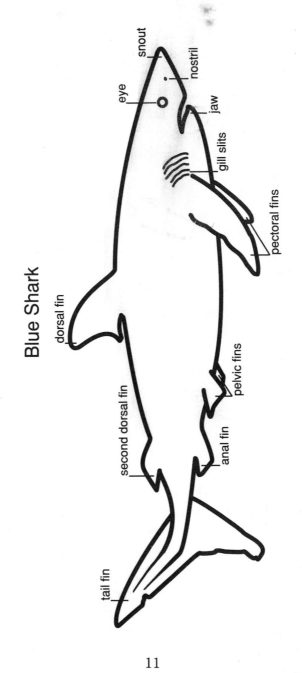

snout

nostril

eye

jaw

gill slits

pectoral fins

dorsal fin

second dorsal fin

pelvic fins

anal fin

tail fin

the water. Blood vessels in the gills take the oxygen to the rest of the shark's body.

Inside a shark's mouth, there are filters that strain the water before it hits the gills. These filters are called gill rakers. Some gill rakers look like stiff bristles. Others look like big pieces of sponge. Like the shark's skeleton, gill rakers are made of cartilage.

Fins

A shark's fins are made of cartilage, too. The tail fin is called the caudal fin. It sweeps back and forth to move the shark forward. Just a few swift waves of the powerful tail will push a shark forward with incredible force.

The stiff fins on the sides of the shark are called pectoral fins. They stick straight out like airplane wings, and they work the same way. A shark can tilt its pectoral fins or move them up and down slightly. By changing their position, the shark steers itself.

Of course a shark is famous for the fin on its back. The dorsal fin, as it is called, is shaped like a triangle and helps a shark keep its balance.

What a shark's fins do not provide is a way of stopping or swimming backward. The side fins on most fish help them to come to a stop. But a shark that is speeding toward something can only turn to keep from crashing. Then it must coast to a stop.

Excellent Swimmers

Nature has given the shark a smooth shape to help it swim. A shark's body looks like a bullet that narrows at both ends. The shark's rounded head lets it move easily through the water, just as an airplane nose helps it glide through the air.

A shark's liver helps it swim, too. The liver is full of oil, and oil is lighter than water. A shark's liver is very large. It can be as much as one quarter of the shark's total weight. Because of its oil-filled liver, the shark weighs less in water and uses less energy as it swims.

Teeth

A shark's teeth may be the most amazing part of its body. Shark teeth wear out and fall out from time to time, but this is not a problem. A shark always has a new supply. Behind the teeth that come out, there are more waiting—rows and rows of them!

A shark's new teeth usually lie flat behind the first row. When a tooth in front is lost, the one behind springs up and moves forward.

Sharks have up to 30 rows of teeth. That means they have as many as 3,000 separate teeth in their mouths at one time! Every two to four weeks, the front row of teeth falls out and a new set moves up. If a shark lives for 30 years, it can use up more than 40,000 teeth!

A shark's teeth don't grow out of a hard jaw-bone, as our teeth do. Instead the teeth sit in soft tissue in the shark's mouth. This makes it easier for the teeth to move around in the mouth and also easier for them to come out. It's not unusual for a shark to swallow its own teeth while it eats.

Different species of sharks have different kinds of teeth. In fact, scientists can look at a tooth and name the kind of shark it came from. One reason for the difference is that certain kinds of teeth are needed to eat certain kinds of food. White sharks have teeth that are thin blades shaped like triangles. These teeth are jagged and good for cutting and tearing off hunks of meat.

The mako and *sand shark* hunt small fish and squid. Their long, thin teeth are better for catching and holding these bite-size animals, which they swallow whole.

Some sharks have flat, blunt teeth that are good for crushing food. The nurse shark is one of these. It feeds on crabs, lobsters, and clams, and needs teeth that can break hard shells.

Some sharks don't need teeth to eat. Instead they use their large gill rakers to strain tiny fish out of the ocean. To feed, they swim slowly through the water with their mouths open. When their gill rakers are full, they swallow. Then they open wide to catch another mouthful of food.

Chapter Three

The Perfect Eating Machine

A shark's body is a finely-tuned food finder. All of the shark's senses help it zero in on the food it needs.

Hearing is often the first sense sharks use to guide them to their prey. A shark has only an inner ear, but it can still hear sounds that are hundreds of yards away. The shark's inner ear is actually a tube that runs under the skin of its head. Sounds are carried along the tube to the shark's brain.

We may think that the deep ocean is a silent place, but it is not. Sea creatures are swimming about. Plants are swishing in the ocean current. Clams are slamming their shells shut. Waves are splashing. Sand is shifting.

Most underwater sounds are pitched too low or too high for our human ears to pick up. Sharks can hear the low-pitched sounds that we miss. A wounded or sick sea creature—the kind of prey that attracts sharks—gives off a low-pitched sound. As a result, a shark knows very quickly where to go for its next meal.

Unfortunately, human beings swimming in water also produce the low pitch that wounded sea creatures make. So sharks are attracted to the sound of humans. This explains why sharks often show up when a plane has crashed in the ocean and is sinking. First they hear the plane hit the water. Then they hear people thrashing in the sea. To a shark, these sounds are very interesting.

Smell

A shark's sense of smell is excellent. And it's no wonder. The section of shark's brain that is used for smelling is as big as the other parts combined!

A shark's sense of smell can even tell if a fish is hurt. How? The shark can smell blood from far away. And if a fish is bleeding, it is usually hurt. If there is only one drop of blood in 100,000,000 drops of water, a shark can smell it. That means the shark knows instantly when a bleeding animal comes within range.

Sharks smell with their nostrils. They do not use their nostrils for breathing, as we do. The nostrils are grooves in the sides of a shark's head. Water flows across the nostril grooves as the shark swims and carries smells to the animal.

Just as certain sounds attract the shark, certain smells excite it, especially the smell of blood.

Vibrating Sense

Let's imagine a shark smells a bleeding fish that has been speared by a diver. The diver is carrying the fish on a string while she looks for other fish to catch. She doesn't know that a shark is following her.

As the shark swims closer, one of its extra senses kicks in. This sense tells the shark more about the speared fish and the diver's movements. The extra sense is a sort of extension of the ears. It lets the shark "feel" noises.

A shark "feels" noise through small canals along the side of its body. These canals are called the lateral line. They are just below the shark's skin and are filled with liquid. The liquid in the canals picks up vibrations. Vibrations in the water are called pressure waves. A shark can feel pressure waves from more than 600 feet away. An injured animal produces a different kind of pressure wave. From these pressure waves, the shark knows where to go to find its prey.

Sight

When the shark is about 50 feet away from the diver, it can see her. Scientists think sharks can see moving objects very well. Sharks can also see patterns such as stripes, and they may see some colors.

A black diving suit covers most of the diver's body. This is lucky because sharks do not seem to see dark colors as well as light ones.

Sharks do seem to be able to see in very little light. This helps them hunt at night and in the dark, deep parts of the ocean. Behind a shark's eyes are silvery plates, like mirrors. The plates reflect light. They also make the shark's eyes glow in the dark as a cat's eyes do.

Touch

Sharks have another special sense that helps them. That sense is touch. Let's go back to the shark that is following the diver. It has been watching what she does. It stays behind the diver to keep from being seen. But when the shark is a few feet away, it comes forward and begins to circle the diver. At last the diver sees the shark.

As the shark circles, it tries to pick up sound or movement signals from the diver. The shark swims in smaller and smaller circles until finally it bumps the diver.

By touching its prey, a shark tries to learn several things. First, it wants to know if the prey will fight back. If the victim does fight, the shark may go away. Sharks usually don't want to fool around with food that might hurt them.

A shark also touches its prey to help it feel the victim's electrical force. A shark can feel the electrical force of animals and objects and even the electromagnetic forces of the earth. The electricity of its prey is one of the last things a shark senses before it attacks.

How does a shark feel this electrical force? The force is felt through pores that cover the outside of a shark's head. The pores or openings lead to little sacs filled with jellylike material. The sacs are connected to nerves. The nerves pick up even the tiniest amount of electricity being given off.

The shark that bumped the diver can feel two electrical forces. One is coming from the diver. The other is coming from the speared fish.

After the diver is bumped by the shark, she hits the shark on the nose with her spear gun. She also drops the fish she is carrying. The shark grabs the fish and swims away. The diver then hurries to escape in the opposite direction. The shark doesn't come after her because it has been hit on the snout. It also has the wounded fish, which is probably what it wanted in the first place.

A Full-Fledged Attack

Let's imagine a *tiger shark* has tracked down a swordfish. It has circled the fish and bumped it. Now it is ready to attack. Many things happen very quickly when a shark attacks.

First the shark opens its jaws, and that movement means several things are happening to the shark's body. The muscles in the shark's neck pull back and lift its long pointed nose. At the same time, its lower jaw juts out. When this happens, the shark's mouth actually moves forward. The mouth is now at the front of the body instead of underneath it. The mouth is in position to attack.

The shark is ready to grab the swordfish. Its mouth is wide open. At the same time, special eyelids slide down over the shark's eyes. These thin white lids protect the shark's eyes while it attacks.

Just before the attack, the shark humps its body into an upside-down U. Then its powerful tail whips out, and the shark springs at the swordfish faster than the eye can see.

The bite comes in two movements. First the lower teeth grab the swordfish. They are sharp spikes that hold on to the prey. Then the muscles that pulled up the upper jaw let go. The snout snaps down like a steel trap closing. The upper teeth sink deep into the swordfish's side.

The shark's bite is powerful for a reason. It has to be strong enough to cut through flesh and break bones. A human jaw is weak by comparison, crunching down at about 150 pounds per square inch. A shark bites down with a force of 44,000 pounds per square inch!

As soon as the tiger shark bites, it shakes it head wildly. The shaking helps the shark's upper teeth saw through the swordfish's body. In no time, the swordfish is nothing but chunks of meat in the shark's stomach.

Feeding Frenzy

If certain kinds of large shark eat the same prey, they may go into what is called a feeding frenzy. No one knows exactly why this happens. We do know that a shark's very sharp senses have a lot to do with it.

Any shark may become excited when it begins to eat. When several sharks are feeding, there are strong smells and noises and sights that excite them. They feel the constant pressure waves made by other sharks. They hear the loud noise of the battle. The sharks begin crowding together, trying to get the next bite. The crowding excites the sharks even more. The more the sharks move around, the more they bump. The more they bump, the more they are jolted by each other's electrical forces.

Soon the sharks are so excited that they begin biting everything around them. They will attack fish, other sharks, people, even boats and anchors. A feeding frenzy is on! Nothing can stop it. Sometimes the sharks twist around and bite themselves.

The frenzy ends as quickly as it began. The sharks have gone a little crazy while trying to fill their stomachs.

A blue shark makes a smooth turn.

To see all around, the hammerhead shark moves its head back and forth as it swims.

The nostrils of the sawshark are found above its eyes.

A lemon shark with remoras attached

This monster-like creature is the horn shark, found in the Pacific Ocean.

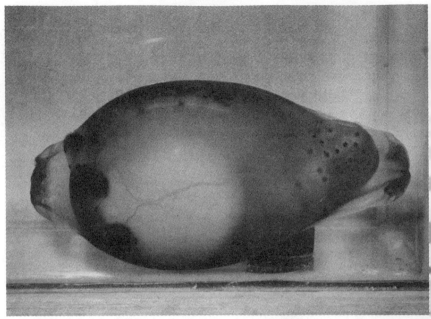

A nurse-shark egg case

This horn-shark egg case was found on a California beach.

A diver studies a tiger shark off the Florida Keys.

Nurse sharks in a "star" grouping

A bonnethead shark with young

The battle-scarred jaws of a great white shark

Like most sharks, the great white has rows of extra teeth.

Marine biologists in Florida study a whale shark.

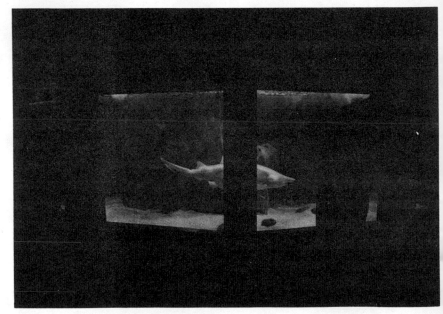

A shark tank at the Mystic Marinelife Aquarium

Chapter Four

What a Shark Eats

Sharks are carnivores. That means they eat meat, such as fish or other sea animals. What sharks don't like is rotten meat. Only if they are starving, will they touch spoiled food.

The largest sharks eat the smallest prey. The whale shark, the basking shark, and the megamouth are the largest of all sharks. They eat plankton, which is a mass of very tiny sea creatures. Plankton grows in bunches and floats in ocean water. A single organism of plankton is so small, you can't see it without a microscope. But plankton is very nourishing when eaten in large amounts.

While many sharks will eat almost anything, others prefer one kind of food. For example, bull sharks like a diet of other sharks. Hammerheads eat mostly stingrays. The *bonnethead shark* prefers shrimp. Nurse sharks like crabs and lobster. The *shortfin mako* looks for bluefish to eat.

31

And the great white shark hunts sea mammals such as seals, sea otters, and whales.

Scientists have discovered that sharks don't eat the same amount of food all the time. Sometimes a shark will eat a lot all at once. People who have caught sharks have found huge amounts of food in their stomachs. A 1,250 pound mako shark was found with 300 pounds of fresh swordfish meat in its stomach. In northern waters, a shark was caught that had swallowed a whole reindeer. Another one had eaten an entire goat, a large turtle, a cat, and three birds. The shark had also swallowed another shark—one that was six feet long!

Sharks can also survive for long periods of time without eating. Great white sharks may be able to live for as long as two months without food. Dr. Eugenie Clark, a famous shark expert, has noticed that nurse sharks tend to lose interest in food when the water turns cold. When they don't eat, sharks live off the oil that's stored in their huge livers.

How much a shark eats may depend on how easy or hard it is for them to find food. This job doesn't seem difficult for the plankton eaters. All they have to do is find plankton and swim through it with their mouths open. However, these sharks can eat a lot of plankton at one time. One basking shark was found with a ton of plankton in its stomach!

The great white shark doesn't eat often. One reason may be that it's harder for a great white to catch the large sea animals it needs to keep its stomach full. When it does find prey, the great white makes one attack and swims away. Then it waits until the animal dies before it returns to finish eating. This way, the white shark is sure its prey won't be able to fight back. But sometimes the prey doesn't die and is able to swim away. Then the great white has to be content with only one bite of a meal.

How much a shark eats might have something to do with how quickly it digests its food. Scientists think a shark may be able to store food for weeks in a certain part of its stomach. If a shark's stomach is full of undigested food, it won't eat.

A normal length of time for a shark to digest a meal is about 24 hours, but sharks can also digest their food faster than that. Once a fisherman caught a large shark that was in the middle of eating a big fish. The tail of the fish was still in the shark's mouth. The head of the fish should have been in the shark's stomach. But the head was already digested. The shark's stomach juices had digested the head before the shark had finished swallowing the fish!

A shark's stomach juices are so strong that they can digest almost anything. The stomach acids of a great white shark can corrode stainless steel. When researchers handle food found in a shark's stomach, they have to wear special gloves. If they don't, the stomach juices will peel the skin right off their hands!

Strange Food

It's a good thing most sharks can digest almost anything because they sometimes gulp down very strange objects. Sharks are curious animals, and they may swallow things by mistake while trying to figure out what they are. Fishermen have found amazing items inside sharks—rolls of tar paper, kegs of nails, car license plates, and even part of a suit of armor.

The tiger shark is also called the garbage-can shark. One tiger shark was found that had swallowed a can of paint, a coil of copper wire, and an eighteen pound drum. Another was found with leather belts, pants, and nine pairs of shoes in its stomach.

Sharks sometimes bite a thing because it looks or acts like food. That is why they have tried to eat underwater telephone cable. When electricity runs through it, the cable seems like a living thing to a shark, and the shark is then likely to attack the cable.

Attacks on Humans

Humans are not a natural food for sharks, but at times sharks attack them anyway. Why would a shark attack a human? One reason is that sharks sometimes think we are the ocean animals or fish that it usually eats. And, as we said earlier, humans make the kinds of sounds that attract sharks. We may also wear colors that attract them.

Some of the first astronauts returning from space found out how quickly sharks respond to noise and to the color orange. When the astronauts' space capsule crashed into the ocean, it made a big splash. The vibrations from the noise attracted many sharks to the landing place.

After the splash down, the astronauts climbed out of the capsule and into life rafts. The rafts were bright orange so that rescuers could spot the astronauts easily. The trouble was that orange was a color sharks could see easily, too. Sharks circled the rafts, making it difficult to pick up the astronauts.

The space program has since made a change. It now uses rafts that are orange on top and black underneath. This way, orange can be seen by rescuers, but the only color beneath the water is black, which does not attract sharks.

A shark attack may also happen because a diver is carrying a camera. Underwater cameras normally have electric flashes on them to shoot pictures in the murky water. The electricity in the camera will attract a shark. However, once the shark has grabbed the camera, it usually leaves the diver alone.

Sometimes a diver may be carrying something that looks like food to a shark. A white diving mask may look like the white belly of a fish to a shark. Metal buckles on a diver's equipment can shine like the silvery scales of a fish.

Sharks may also attack a diver who has entered their territory. Humans are simply not welcome where sharks live, eat, and have their babies.

Hunger, too, may be a reason that sharks attack humans. No one knows whether or not a shark likes the taste of a human, but taste may not matter if a shark is very hungry. Still, the chances of a person being attacked by a shark are very, very small.

Out of almost 400 kinds of sharks, only about 30 species are at all dangerous to humans. Most of these attack only when they have been disturbed. Only three kinds of sharks tend to attack swimmers. The three most dangerous sharks are great white sharks, tiger sharks, and bull sharks.

Each year, only about 100 people around the world are attacked by sharks. Of that number, only twenty of them die from the attack. More people than that are killed each year in automobile accidents on the way to the beach.

Chapter Five

Shark Babies

There is still a lot we don't know about sharks, especially the way they reproduce. Most sharks mate and give birth in parts of the ocean where humans can't watch. We do know that some species mate in the spring. We know that some sharks play special games with each other before they mate. For example, *lemon sharks* do a gentle underwater ballet together before they mate.

Some mating play is not gentle. Many male sharks bite the females during mating. These bites heal quickly, but they sometimes leave scars on the females. Even so, female sharks don't really have to worry about being hurt. Females are usually bigger and stronger than males. A female shark can kill a male if he hurts her too much.

The male shark has a mating organ called a clasper. When two sharks are mating, the male fits his clasper into an opening in the female, called a vent. Then the male's sperm travels through the vent to fertilize the eggs inside the female.

When the baby sharks are born, they are perfectly formed. Baby sharks are called pups. They look just like their parents, only smaller. From birth, their eyes, nostrils, ears, and feeling senses are well developed. Their teeth are sharp. Shark pups are ready to hunt and eat as soon as they are born.

Sharks That Hatch From Eggs

Baby sharks are born in three different ways. The first is by hatching from an egg laid by the mother. These sharks are called oviparous. Only a few kinds of sharks are oviparous. These include whale sharks, hornsharks, and cat sharks.

Soon after mating, the oviparous mother shark drops her eggs in the water and swims away. Each egg has a sac around it that hardens until it is as tough as leather. The sac works like armor to protect the egg. The sacs are sometimes called mermaid's purses because they look like handbags.

The mother drops her egg sacs in a place where the babies will have a good chance to grow. The sacs quickly anchor themselves to something for protection. Some sacs have dangling strings that help them catch onto seaweed.

Other sacs are sticky and fasten easily onto rocks.

Inside the sac is the unborn baby shark, called an embryo. The sac also contains a yolk, which is the embryo's food. After a certain number of months, the baby shark hatches.

The second group of shark babies also hatches from eggs. But these eggs hatch inside the mothers. Instead of strong sacs, the eggs have thin shells around them. These sharks are called ovoviviparous. Ovoviviparous sharks include tiger sharks, makos, and great whites.

After the eggs hatch inside the mother, the embryos feed first on a yolk and then on a rich, creamy liquid. The embryos may grow inside the mother for many months before they are born.

Sharks Born Like Mammals

The third group of shark babies does not hatch from eggs. The embryos have no sac or shell to protect them. Instead, they grow inside the mother the same way human babies do. A cord forms between the mother and the baby. Food passes from the mother to the baby through the cord. This third group of sharks is called viviparous. Some viviparous species are hammerheads, basking sharks, and lemon sharks.

These sharks need a long time to develop inside the mother before the babies are born. Scientists know that a lemon shark takes one year to develop inside its mother. A *spiny dogfish shark* needs two years to grow before it is born.

In some cases scientists are sure which species of sharks hatch eggs inside the mothers and which don't. But in other cases scientists are still not sure. It is difficult information to gather because researchers have not been able to examine many pregnant females. And they have not seen many sharks giving birth. The sharks we do know about are the ones that can survive in aquariums or live in shallow waters.

Lemon sharks are a good species for researchers to study. For one thing, they always return to the same place to have their babies. Like most viviparous sharks, they give birth to their live babies in shallow water.

Lemon pups stay in the shallow lagoons for the first years of their lives. Until they're grown, they are safer here than they would be in the open ocean. They also like shallow water because it is warm.

Many baby lemon sharks live in a lagoon together, but each one has its own special area, called an activity space. The pups don't seem to care if their activity space overlaps with another pup's. They never fight over their space or try to keep other pups out. As the baby gets bigger, its activity space gets bigger, too. When lemon sharks are about five years old, they leave the shallows for deep water.

Many kinds of sharks group together for the first few years of their lives. When they become adults, some stay in schools, and others swim off by themselves.

Chapter Six

Friends and Enemies

There are two small fish that like the shark's company—the pilot fish and the remora. Swimming close to the shark gives these small creatures protection from larger fish. But the main reason they stay near is because the shark is a messy eater. When a sharks tears into food, bits always scatter in the water. The pilot and remora pick up the crumbs.

Pilot fish are about two feet long. Some have beautiful blue stripes. Others are black and yellow. They usually swim above a shark, like guards. It was once thought that a shark had bad eyesight. People said the striped fish were pilots that guided the shark. That's how the fish got its name. People said the shark was so grateful that it didn't eat the pilot fish.

We now know that sharks have excellent eyesight and don't need a guide. In fact, they would probably eat the pilot fish, but the small fish seem to be too quick to catch.

The pilot fish does not do anything for the shark, but the remora does perform a service. It cleans the shark by eating tiny parasites which dig into the shark's skin.

Remoras can be a few inches long, or they can grow to three feet in length. They may be red, green or gray. The remora has an interesting way of traveling. On the top of its head is a flat oval pad of strong suckers. Thanks to the suckers, the remora can attach itself to fish, turtles, or even boats. Often it sticks itself onto a shark and rides along with its big host.

A Shark's Enemies

One enemy of the shark can be another shark. Big sharks will sometimes eat smaller sharks. Healthy sharks may eat weak or hurt sharks. A shark that is hooked by a fisherman is sometimes eaten by another shark before the fisherman can get his trophy out of the water. Once a man caught a large tiger shark. He opened up its stomach and found a smaller bull shark inside. In the bull shark's stomach was a *blacktip shark,* and inside the blacktip was a dogfish shark!

There seem to be no real rules about sharks attacking each other. Researchers think that some of the attacks are accidental. However, scientists do know that a shark won't attack a member of its own species if it is the same size. That is why sharks that swim together in schools tend to be the same size. They will not attack each other, and the size of the school protects them from larger sharks. Sharks seem to be very good at judging each others' sizes. A dogfish shark, for example, will not swim with a dogfish that is more than 7 percent larger than itself.

Does a shark have other enemies? Very few. A giant squid is an enemy. Alligators and crocodiles can also kill a shark that swims too close to their river homes.

A porpoise looks playful, but it can kill a shark. However, the porpoise is not a meat eater, and it doesn't kill a shark for food. Porpoises kill sharks only to protect themselves.

A shark may go after a baby porpoise or a wounded adult. When this happens, the adult porpoises gang up on the shark. They ram the shark's tender stomach, trying to crush its insides. Or they butt against the shark's gills so that it can't breathe.

One dangerous enemy of the shark is the killer whale. Like sharks, these black-and-white whales are meat eaters. And shark meat is one of their favorite foods.

Killer whales are bigger than most sharks, even makos and the great whites. Makos are about twelve feet long. Great whites run about fifteen feet in length. Killer whales can grow to be 30 feet long. So they can attack almost any shark they come across. One killer whale was seen holding a nine-foot shark in its mouth.

A shark's worst enemies are people. Before there was electricity, people hunted sharks for their oil. The oil was burned in lamps. People also wanted shark oil because it was rich in vitamin A.

Today, we still hunt sharks. We now use shark oil to make oil paints and to grease machinery. Shark teeth are mounted in gold or silver and made into earrings and necklaces. And sharkskin is being used to make leather shoes, belts, and handbags. Other parts of the shark's body are used for fertilizer. But the main reason sharks are hunted is for food.

In recent years, the demand for shark meat has increased all over the world. Unfortunately, fishing companies are not always careful about how many sharks they kill. The United States government and people who study sharks are worried. They say if we don't reduce shark fishing, some species will be in danger of extinction.

Are Sharks Endangered?

The spiny dogfish shark is one species that may already be endangered. Millions and millions of pounds of dogfish shark are sold each year for food. Many of these sharks are caught in the Atlantic Ocean near the northeast United States. There are so many being caught in this area by fishing companies from various nations that soon there may be no more to catch. This has already happened to the spiny dogfish in other parts of the world.

Some sharks are being destroyed just for their fins. Fins are the most valuable part of a shark. In Oriental countries, they are used to make a very popular shark fin soup. After Japanese and other fishermen catch the sharks, they cut off their fins and throw the sharks back into the water. This kind of fishing is called finning. Finning is cruel because the definned sharks cannot swim and soon die.

Fishing fleets kill thousands of sharks at a time. Some fishing companies use airplanes to spot schools of sharks. Once a school is found, the fishing boats come with huge nets to scoop up the sharks.

The danger is that we are fishing faster than the sharks can reproduce. Sharks aren't able to have babies fast enough to replace the ones that are killed. For example, the spiny dogfish shark isn't able to reproduce at all until it is *fifteen* years old. Even then, it only gives birth to about five pups every two years.

Some people kill sharks because the sharks are costing them money. For example, cod fishing companies in Newfoundland kill the large basking sharks that become tangled in the cod nets. During their migrations each year, these giants swim near shore and destroy thousands of dollars worth of fishing equipment.

Killing sharks for sport is a favorite American hobby. To many people, deep-sea shark fishing is very exciting. Sharks fight hard to get off the hook. A huge mako will leap fifteen or twenty feet out of the water trying to get free. A great white shark is considered the most thrilling catch of all. It is possible that the big sport-fishing sharks will be fished to death.

The loss will be great if any shark species dies out. Sharks play an important part in keeping nature in balance. If they disappear, the balance will be disturbed.

Nature uses many systems to make sure life survives. Sharks have their place in these systems. One system is called the food cycle. In the food cycle, every animal and plant is food for another living thing. In the ocean, the tiny floating plankton feed fish big and small. The small fish are eaten by larger fish. Then the large fish are eaten by predators such as sharks and killer whales.

When a shark dies, its body is partly eaten by other predators. The rest falls to the bottom of the ocean and feeds the starfish and crabs. What is left decays and turns into minute bits of food for plankton. Then the cycle is ready to begin again.

Different species of sharks also help the balance of nature by eating different kinds of food. If all sharks ate crabs, for example, there would soon be no crabs left. The food web would be damaged. But when nature is in balance, the food web stays intact.

Nature has another system to make sure living creatures survive. This system is called the survival of the fittest. By being predators, sharks actually help other species to stay strong.

Sharks usually go after the weakest animals because these are the easiest to catch. By going after weak or injured creatures, the shark is leaving stronger animals alone. The strong, healthy animals then have more space and more food. With better living conditions, they become even healthier. They also have healthier babies.

Many people still believe that sharks are bad or evil creatures. They think the shark's purpose in life is to hurt human beings. Of course this is not true, but people are slow to change their ideas. What will help is education. The more we learn about these creatures, the sooner everyone will understand that the shark has a valuable place in nature.

Chapter Seven

Studying Sharks

Sharks are not easy animals to study. Many live in places that are hard to get to. Another problem is that many sharks are rovers. They swim great distances every year. Their constant movement makes them difficult to find and difficult to watch.

Researchers study some kinds of sharks in aquariums. And there are certain species that thrive in captivity. Unfortunately, other sharks cannot live long in aquarium tanks. You will rarely see a great white, mako, tiger or blacktip shark in an aquarium. If they are captured, they soon stop eating. They rub and bang the walls of the tank until their skin is raw. Eventually they die.

The nurse, lemon, *sand tiger*, and leopard sharks are some of the ones that can adjust to living in tanks. These sharks swim on the ocean floor or in shallow waters near the shore. Their homes are full of rock ledges and coral reefs. As a result, these sharks can become used to living in a tank with walls around them.

Dr. Eugenie Clark has studied sharks in tanks for many years. She was one of the first researchers to do experiments on shark intelligence.

First Dr. Clark trained some sharks to ring a bell for their dinners. Then she put two targets in the shark pond at her laboratory. One target was attached to a bell. The other wasn't. If the sharks bumped the target with the bell, they would get food.

After a few weeks, the sharks in the test had learned to ring only the bell target. The best student turned out to be a baby nurse shark. It pressed the right target every time after only five days.

Many experiments are being performed on sharks in captivity. However, some of the tests may not be accurate. This is because the sharks being tested are living in a tank, a place that is unnatural. They may act differently in a tank than they would in the open ocean. The best place to study sharks is in the ocean, but how can that be done?

Tagging

One good way to study sharks in ocean water is by using a method called tagging. The famous underwater explorer Jacques Cousteau used the tagging method. Members of his crew went underwater while inside a steel shark cage. When sharks swam close to the cage, the divers shot brightly-colored tags into the sharks' fins.

On the tags there were instructions in five different languages. They asked the person who found the tag to mail it back to the researchers. Using tags, scientists can tell how far sharks travel and where they go. Thanks to one tag, researchers learned that a blue shark swam three thousand miles — across the Atlantic Ocean, from the United States to Africa.

Tagging also tells researchers how much sharks grow. A tag can help them learn about the lifespan of sharks. One *sandbar shark* was captured nineteen years after it was tagged!

Dr. Samuel Gruber has tagged thousands of lemon sharks in the ocean off Miami, Florida. Dr. Gruber tags his sharks by hand. His crew catches a shark on a fishing hook or with ropes. Dr. Gruber carefully cuts a slit in the shark's back, just below the dorsal fin. Then he puts in a flat triangle made of stainless steel. A tube is attached to the triangle. Inside the tube is a waterproof tag with a number on it and Dr. Gruber's address.

This kind of shark tagging doesn't hurt the animal. The cut heals quickly.

Lemon sharks are members of the largest family of sharks. What Dr. Gruber and other scientists learn about them can be applied to many other sharks. And because lemon sharks always return to the same place to have their pups, scientists are able to check the same shark many times over its lifespan.

Studying Speed

John McClosker is a famous great white shark expert. He studies great whites all over the world. One of the questions he asked about sharks was: "How fast does a great white swim?" To answer that, he attached paddle wheels to the back of several great whites. As the sharks swam through the water, McClosker measured how fast each wheel turned. By doing this, he was able to judge how fast a shark travelled. He could also tell how often the shark stopped and how much it speeded up when it attacked.

McClosker was amazed to discover that the great white shark is a slow swimmer. It moves only one mile an hour when gliding around the ocean. Even when it is chasing food, it reaches a speed of only three miles an hour. In comparison, a human being who swims well can reach a speed of almost four miles an hour!

Sam Gruber, another scientist, found that the lemon shark is also a slow poke. Its normal rate is only one mile per hour. When it is pursuing food, the shark speeds up to only one and a half miles per hour.

Sharks are cruisers. They glide in the water as much as possible in order to use up as little energy as they can. Only when they go for food, do they turn on the steam. Some sharks, when they attack, can move as fast as 40 miles per hour.

Radios and Subs

Radio transmitters also help scientists study sharks. John McClosker often attaches transmitters to the great white sharks he studies. A transmitter sends messages back to the research crew in their boat and helps them follow the shark.

Using transmitters has some problems, however. The researchers can't always tell the difference between the sounds of the transmitter and other noises in the ocean.

Many scientists now observe sharks from a submersible. A submersible is a tiny submarine. Usually it is only big enough for a few people and some equipment. Many of these subs can dive 4,500 feet deep.

Dr. Eugenie Clark now uses submersibles to study deep-sea sharks. In earlier years, she tried catching the deep-water swimmers. But when she brought them up to the surface, the sharks died. The surface of the water was much warmer than the cool ocean bottom. Dr. Clark decided the sharks couldn't adjust to the warm temperature. Using submersibles, she and other shark experts can go down to observe sharks without hurting them.

The most recent findings about sharks have been very interesting. After a fair amount of study, researchers think the cartilage in a shark's body prevents it from getting cancer. Scientists now hope that shark cartilage may be used to help stop cancer in humans as well.

Study a Living Shark

Would you like to see a shark? You don't have to go out into the ocean to see one. There are many aquariums around the country that have sharks. There might be one near you where you can see several shark species. You can see how they swim and use their fins. You can look at the way they feed and maybe get a chance to see the jaw move forward when they bite.

Here is a list of good aquariums:

Baltimore Aquarium, Baltimore, MD

Miami Seaquarium, Miami, FL

Mote Marine Laboratory, Sarasota, FL

Mystic Marinelife Aquarium, Mystic, CT

New England Aquarium, Boston, MA

New York Aquarium, Brooklyn, NY

Seaworld, Orlando, FL

Seaworld, San Diego, CA

Shedd Aquarium, Chicago, IL

Steinhart Aquarium, San Francisco, CA